WRITING YOUR NAME ON THE GLASS

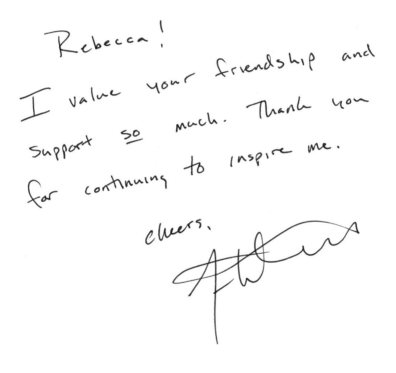

Rebecca!
I value your friendship and
support so much. Thank you
for continuing to inspire me.

Cheers,

EDITORS' SELECTION FROM
THE 2018 FROST PLACE CHAPBOOK COMPETITION

WRITING YOUR NAME ON THE GLASS

POEMS

JIM WHITESIDE

BULL★CITY
PRESS

DURHAM, NORTH CAROLINA

Writing Your Name on the Glass

Editors' Selection from the 2018 Frost Place Chapbook Competition

Published in the United States of America

Library of Congress Cataloging-in-Publication Data

Whiteside, Jim
Writing Your Name on the Glass: poems / by Jim Whiteside
p.   cm.
ISBN-13: 978-1-949344-08-0

Book design by Spock and Associates with Callie Riek
Cover photo by Barney Moss
Author photo by Adam Sikora

Published by
BULL CITY PRESS
1217 Odyssey Drive
Durham, NC 27713

www.BullCityPress.com

CONTENTS

*

WRITING YOUR NAME ON THE GLASS

LITTLE FUGUE

Sometimes, the memory of him playing
runs backwards. The notes leave the room, return
to the end of his instrument, back to his body.

I close my eyes and see him making reeds
at his workbench. He sharpens the knife
on the spinning wheel, the blade glowing.

The first time I knelt for a man, my hands shook,
reaching for his waistline. His smooth torso shone.
The moon in the window was a fully-clenched fist.

Shaping the cane, he shapes the notes themselves.
He ties up each mouthpiece with a length
of thread, singeing the ends with a match.

MORNING SONG

Feathered thing   un-pinnable, un-

cageable, when I say   *You are many-sided*

as a cut diamond,   I mean

Your hands for doing, your   wide wingspan, your

always open mouth. Stippled pond   half-frozen over,

little bead of sea   glass, when I say   *The daffodils*

are foolish, I mean   Late frost—sheathed in ice,

brittle as glass. You know   these things already,

I'm an easy tell.   I can't help I'm the kind of boy

born with his heart   on the outside, hard

for me to help   what you can and cannot see.

HELD TO THE WALL, DRIVEN AS A NAIL

He approached love, my body, his
as a painter his easel, the role

of maker, the nerve to say, *Let's make*
something from nothing, I'll push around

some pigment and make a face. Cold, I paced
the house in his sweater. The pictures

on the walls tracked me with their eyes.
They say the great discovery is that

of the lover's body, the way they must be
touched, how to love them properly.

But what if it is less discovery
and more command—*touch me here,*

and here, and here—the body schematic?
This is what I came to see as love:

a kind of servitude, taking the shape
of another's design. To give in.

PARABLE

He shaved his head to plant
    the hair in his garden, said

        I'll make something
grow. Held his hands, his curved fingers

        as if to cup light. For weeks he didn't
        eat, for weeks we never

spoke, never touched. Heart with
    a hole in it. Hand that drops

        the stone it holds. He shaved
his arms because he liked

    the way they moved
        through the air, smooth

and mechanical. I dreamed
    he grew so thin all his clothes

        fell off, I dreamed
his mouth full of suns,

    I dreamed he called my name
        to the room's farthest corners.

Once, he told me about
    hunting with his father,

        its strange beauty.
How the word dress means

    to adorn oneself, but also
        for everything to be stripped

away, to be hung
    by the foot on a hook.

OPEN

your mouth past any jaw's

unhinging   spread like drying flowers

petal by petal   unblooming

We lived for months in silence   and without

touching   *My skin* I thought   *is like a wall*

good for keeping in and keeping out   When

I opened the window   I invited only wind

but with it came   a scattering of leaves

shield-shaped bug, a layer of pollen   We lived

looking away from our faces   paced the halls

and took turns   being the ghost

And what will you do when   even the specter

of me is gone   Will the dust praise you

What truth of yours   could it sing

GOLDBERG VARIATIONS

these hands, their roughness
if you tell me what to swallow, I'll do it

    sheathed in ice, brittle as glass
another kind of groping in the dark

    a blue note fills the room
climb on top, again and again

what the mouth means
he commands the leaves to fall

    smell of sweat, breath like creosote
sifting desert sand through fingers

    roots turn back to dirt
trees left with their nakedness

voice like a trombone's slide
the weight of one body on another

    moves from one pitch to the next
he who holds the gun

    the way we learn language
he who churns the waters

what the mouth means when it speaks
smell of cologne—a man wants to touch me

turn to ash, turn to bone
I'm trying to unhinge my jaw

speak, speak
my mouth full of rust

VESSEL

Clutch   of geese cross the pond,

gosling like a machine   the kind of boat

that's designed to barely disturb the surface.

What the ceiling fan doesn't do   I'll do

with my wings,   cloud of feathers.

When he told me he couldn't hold me   close

enough, I tried   to get closer,   close

as a straight-razor shave   exposed neck

the sharpening blade   the strop.   My sister

she told me   to hold my breath as we

drove past the graveyard   I didn't listen.

I'm only looking for some square   of light

to pray in,   my body full of lightning

at the touch. I'm only looking   for a way

to end this battle   this war is not new

just the body, again   broken & burning.

AMERICAN SEABED

—Dario Robleto; mixed media with butterflies and fossilized
whale ear bones; 2014

1.

In the telling, sometimes also a warning.
The rock split in two, and then there was
water. The body is also a container—
and hear this, little bird, there are many men
who will try to break you. Here,
with his foot to the wall, one with a shock
of white hair packs his cigarettes
against his palm. The body is a container
as a drum is a skin pulled tight. He loves you
and could never love you, his hand
on your back the worst part of his memory.

2.

I went to the greenhouse and all the plants
had died. The cacti had yellowed,
and the large forsythia turned brittle.
In my reflection I saw him standing next
to me, saying something I could not
make out, as if yelled through water.
The moon Cheshired, every one of his teeth
visible in the glass. Wind and more wind,
and what else? Some winged thing
against my eardrum, saying, *Closer, come closer still.*

TAME

Seeing the bared teeth of one chained

to the tree, we say *The animal must*

be trained. But what of me?
                              What I found

in the body of the first lover: a lost gospel

preaching wildness. *It must be broken,* we say

when the animal is too much an animal,

and opening my body to his body also felt like

a breaking.
              In those days, repair meant

sitting at the edge of the fountain

tossing coins. With each, the wish I might learn

which is greater: the lark's extended wing,

the trees' shifting shadows, the birds

that peck and flutter at our feet in the plaza,

the ghosts inside us, unchained, waiting.

WRITING YOUR NAME ON THE GLASS

Again in a stranger's living room, I wait to get my hands beneath his clothes, in his hair, this man with a tight, smooth body, his muscles electric, a dancer, his body moving through the room like a machine, practiced and studied movements.

And again, a man who will not trust anything he can not hold in his hands. He lives alone and in a clean space, says, *No living thing is in here but me, not a dog, not a plant.*

I sleep in his arms, the fanblades spinning overhead a quiet continuous rhythm.

*

I sat on the park bench for a long time, waiting to wake up, watching the bees fly around, pollinating the world.

I thought my life would be different—we all thought our lives would be at least a little different.

The warehouse across the street, all boarded up, they say might make a nice grocery store, brimming with colorful fruit and fresh-cut flowers, glass cases full of choices and glowing beautiful light.

*

Today, I've catalogued my interactions: clerks behind counters, short exchanges, paper bags and paper smiles.

It's the kind of love I'm afraid I'm best at—brief but hopeful—a smiling man on a small illuminated screen says he wants me to dominate him.

He's only half a mile away, and I already have such love for all of him, as if every man I've ever held close is the utterance of the same broken prayer.

*

I'm still here, writing these lines about light and love, still sitting on the shower floor, watching the water pool and drain, still writing your name on the glass shower door, watching the steam erase it slowly.

*

Here's what I remember—reaching in the dark, days and nights, the only light in the room from the open refrigerator, your silhouette.

You said, *You're like a pumpkin, hollow and without a heart.* and I felt it.

I said I would meet you in the square, and you waited for hours.

I got lost in the park looking at plants and thinking about grace.

You waited for me, just sat there and waited until I showed up, my mind full of all those open-throated flowers, everything with its own energy and light and life, even the struck crow on the road, three wing feathers standing up, shaking slightly in the wind—

*

I wake in the bleach-bright room with the doctor prodding my arm, asking how many men I've touched, and when, and how.

And how I stay so thin.

I tell him about the holding, after, about the sunglasses one man left in my car, about bathroom floors paved with subway tile, places worn thin, chips and cracks.

I do not tell him about your smile, your ever-flowing patience.

I tell him, instead, about ice skating, my bruised hip another man said looked like a late Rothko—thin and purple and delicate.

LETTER FOR THE MUSICIAN

In the dream where
you have not yet left

me, we are talking
about the cosmos again.

Not the useless
science of planetary

alignments, houses,
and constellations, but

the realities of the universe.
Distances so great we

measure them by tracking
the way light travels.

You say, *There are stars*
the size of this city

and a thousand times
denser than lead,

small dying things who,
in their final millennia

turn themselves to metal
in their desperation.

We're sitting on the bay
window seat. A wren lands

on the feeder. Your mouth
opens and the building staccato

of *Symphony in C*
bursts forth, every note

struck perfectly.
In a moment, we appear

in space, and we are orbiting
some distant star, not

our own. Your mouth stays
open, though in the place

of sound comes a spiral
cloud of black feathers.

FLAME

The air in your mouth I've felt is fire.

Tell me your age in ringed circles, in cracked earth, tell me
    your drought,
        grackle-throated love, fan-plume.

Here in desert cities we need so many more water towers,
        everything your shadow touches you can claim
            as your own war.

When the captain says *Safety off* he means fire
        he means *at will*.

Hold me in your hand like a bird
        or something else that can't be trusted.

AFTERLOVE

Then there was the time I felt the room I was in
a prison: the young squirrel my childhood cat caught

and let go inside our house: a blur, all tail,
and my mother's screams for a more favorable

catch-and-release. The way I held it—firm
but not so tight as to bruise—how readily my hands

became a cage, such utility. Once, I picked up a man

at a bar—while he slept a blue light from the bathroom
illuminated part of his body. How long I spent studying

his lone tattoo: a fly wing, in such detail, above his heart.

MORNING SONG

You be the rock I salt   my tongue with

be the blade slid beneath the nail   the nail

driven too deeply in the wood, haloed,   morning's

first   steps in wet grass.

Turned on her back, the spider   reveals her

poison,   fiery belly.   In the battlefield

the officers, too, agree   *There's more than one way*

to win this war.   Our home front: coalblack hands, rough

stone in the pocket   worried smooth.

FUGUE

We ran from the back door,
    laughing, set little fires

        all over the city, small
ignitions, watched them burn.

    Told me he worked best
        at night, slept all day. Held

lightning in his hands, threw
    bolts. Told me *There must be*

        a place for us in this
world. We'll find it and build

    a wall around it. Made music,
        sang like a bird or a stone

dropped in a well. Filled
    my mouth with fig blossoms,

        coated my throat with ash.
Field I planted with spring

    melons, field which got no
        rain, empty bowl. Even now

I toss with dreams
    of the guns he kept

        so clean, oiled. I think
What if each bullet were

        an olive pit? I think *What if*
            his hands were doves?

DISGUISE GAME

Strange embrace. The throat's   soft bleating.

I wake in the forest   dreaming of the forest,

studying the lake   reflecting the trees.

I've played this game before,   the one that goes

I'll be the wolf, and you be   *the sheepskin I hide in.*

You taught it to me   some time ago. Take

what you will, and take it   with salted tongue.

Stay quiet—   I've always known you best

through your actions   silent.

CENTO

The boy walked away
      with a flock of cranes following him
              like Sonny Liston
         with an open fist.
I wanted
      to reflect the sun; I kept praying. Dolls
         exist, dreamers and dolls;
killers exist, and doves, and doves.

I look at my body under the spell
            of gravity:
      a split fig, filled with dew, and

         if I could live again
as just one thing, it would be
      the forgotten trap he set—the mock blood,
this begging, a decade of stones
              inside me still.

NOTES AND ATTRIBUTIONS

"Little Fugue" borrows a phrase from Eduardo C. Corral's poem "Want" from his collection *Slow Lightning*, and is written as a response to that poem.

"Morning Song (Feathered thing...)" borrows a phrase from the album *The Always Open Mouth* by the experimental rock band Fear Before.

"Open:" Psalm 30:9: "What gain is there in my death? Will the dust praise you? Will it proclaim Your truth?"

"Goldberg Variations" is for Ashley Griffeth, who helped me arrive at one of the lines. The poem references the song "Tell Me What To Swallow" by the experimental electronic duo Crystal Castles.

"Vessel:" The final couplet owes much to my reading of the work of Matt Rasmussen and Kate Daniels.

"Cento:" Thanks, respectively, to W. S. Merwin, Rick Hilles, Jericho Brown, Inger Christensen, Alicia Ostriker, Bruce Snider, Beth Bachmann, Richard Siken.

ACKNOWLEDGEMENTS

Thanks to the editors of the following journals for publishing the poems in this manuscript, some either in earlier drafts or versions:

The Adroit Journal: "Morning Song (Feathered thing...)"

Crazyhorse: "Flame" and "Tame"

The Journal: "Fugue"

Lumina: "Parable"

The Massachusetts Review: "Goldberg Variations"

Ninth Letter: "Afterlove" (as "Saudade")

PANK Magazine: "Little Fugue"

Pleiades: "Writing Your Name on the Glass"

Poetry Northwest: "American Seabed"

Post Road: "Cento"

Redivider: "Open"

Salt Hill Journal: "Morning Song (You be the rock...)" and "Vessel"

SLICE Magazine: "Held to the Wall, Driven as a Nail" and "Letter for the Musician"

The Southern Review: "Disguise Game"

*

I owe many thanks to many people for their support of the writing of these poems.

Thank you to the kind faculty at Vanderbilt University and The University of North Carolina at Greensboro, for showing the way.

I'm grateful for a residency at The Virginia Center for the Creative Arts, where many of these poems were first drafted, and a scholarship from The Sewanee Writer's Conference, where I received invaluable encouragement, help, and fellowship.

To all of my friends, thank you—particularly Colby Cotton and Michael Pontacoloni, for keeping my fire fueled; Jacques J. Rancourt, for your encouragement; and Chloe Anne Campbell, for being my first and best reader.

Thanks to Noah Stetzer and Ross White at Bull City Press for believing in this project. This chapbook's success owes a great deal to Noah's sharp editorial guidance and Ross's vision for design and layout.

Thanks to my parents, Jim and Pauline Whiteside, for understanding the writing life. And thank you to Cody Risinger, for believing in me.

ABOUT THE AUTHOR

Jim Whiteside's poems have received support from
The Sewanee Writers' Conference, The Virginia
Center for the Creative Arts, and The University of
North Carolina at Greensboro, where he earned his
MFA. His poems have appeared in journals such
as *The Southern Review, Crazyhorse, Washington
Square Review,* and *Salt Hill,* as winner of the Philip
Booth Poetry Prize. Originally from Cookeville,
Tennessee, he lives in Madison, Wisconsin, where he
works as a copywriter and as a staff member for *The
Adroit Journal.*